Quit Your Job or Die

Discover the Importance of Self-Employment

Booklocker.com, Inc.
2010

Quit Your Job or Die

Discover the Importance of Self-Employment

Joshua Tolley

Edited by Kimberly Leinstock

This book is dedicated to my parents, and my brothers who make me a better person. Kim, with her endless talent, made this whole book legible and a joy to work on.

I also want to dedicate this book to Jeff Mosurinjohn. His influence on me, both in business and in life, has left an impact that will last a lifetime. Those who are blessed with his friendship are blessed indeed.

Table of Contents

Introduction

Odds are you have a job. I'm sorry. My condolences go out to you, your family, and your friends. There is no such thing as "job security." If you are employed by another person and you are making even $300,000 per year, you are broke (money with no freedom is just as broke as freedom with no money). The odds of you getting a divorce and/or having other family problems are astronomical. And your ability to make an impact on your family name (in a positive way) is pretty much non-existent. Matter of fact, if you are under the age of 60 and employed, chances are you will actually die at your place of employment. (Just like you always dreamed, I'm sure.) The reason I wrote this book is because when it comes down to it, I don't want you to die without having the best life possible.

There are millions of people, who due to fate have very little control over their situation—the mentally handicapped, the infirmed, those who live in nations without freedom, and those who died "too young."

Here you are, obviously, not dead, able to read, think, and reason. You probably don't have a debilitating condition. This means you do have control over the situation, control over the course your life takes. The question is, why are you not living the life you are capable of living? Why do you choose to suck up to your boss as opposed to take that dream vacation or live in that dream home?

There are too many mothers and fathers who die without spending enough quality time with their children. An untold number of people suffer depression, alcohol and drug use by the onset of stress caused by employment and lack of money. Around you there are bucket lists without check marks, broken relationships left broken, and too many people living in situations that they would not live in if they had the choice. The list goes on and on, but you get the point.

Look, let's be honest. There are going to be "experts" who will say this book is just a load of bull crap. Let the "experts" come, because at the end of the day all that really matters is how well you sleep at night. If this book helps one person find a path to a life filled with time, money, freedom, and great relationships, it is worth all the worthless criticism this book may bring.

Don't spend what little time you have left in this world wasting it. You don't get a "do over" and there is only security found in risk (that's deep, too deep for an intro).

Every minute you have left is valuable. Every choice you make will either take you further from or closer to the life you want. With that in mind, take down your defenses; there is nobody here except for you and me. No need to hold on to ego or status, no need to get defensive. Instead, read the book. Look at yourself and the world around you. Think logically without prejudice and you will find this to be one of the most liberating experiences of your life (so far).

Chapter One:

Forbes 400

When I was in school, I had a rough time. The details don't matter as much as what I discovered, so suffice it to say, school and I did not see eye to eye. How does this relate to the Forbes 400? Well, I'm glad you asked. One day I noticed the teachers were instructing me and my fellow students the way to make sure you have a successful and happy life. I thought this instruction was kind of odd since they were telling a few hundred unique individuals ONE way to happiness. How on earth can one path lead to happiness for hundreds of people with different dreams, wants, talents, desires, and opportunities? It cannot.

So what was this one answer they were giving to all of us? Go to college, get good grades, get a good job and that will give you a good life. That was it. Looking back at that now I realize that NONE of the things that make a good life and certainly nothing that makes a great life is in their equation. Where is the purpose and passion? Where's the happiness found in having a great home life with family? Where was the adventure in exploring your potential? Love, where is the love, for goodness sake?

As their instruction played over and over again in my head, it was like walking into my home and noticing something is a bit "off," but I just couldn't tell what it was, like a crooked picture on the wall. For about 3 days, I couldn't figure it out.

(For the sake of protecting the innocent, we will call my teacher "Mr. Smith".)

I found myself walking through a grocery store and my mom asked me to find some pasta. So like any good son, I embark on my mission. Not finding what I am looking for I do what every man does, I stop and ask for directions.

Walking past the meat department, I see a store worker. You know the look: the paper hat, the shirt with a name tag and that classic apron. I say, "Excuse me, sir. Can you help me?" Mr. Smith (my teacher) turns around, and he has the look of a sad little dog as he says, "The pasta is down isle 3, and it's on sale this week."

That was it! That's the crooked picture on the wall! Mr. Smith and everyone who did what Mr. Smith was instructing us to do to have a great life had, in fact, the kind of life I never want.

(Now, just let me make something very clear here. I have great respect for Mr. Smith. It takes a real man to swallow his pride and take on a very honorable job in a grocery store to make ends meet for his family. While not a good example of how to achieve victory at that time, he was a perfect example of how to step up to the plate and be a real man. If any women are reading this and your husband, who you have been disappointed in, is taking on "low" jobs to make sure the family is warm and fed, grow up and be happier [notice I said happi_er_] with your man. I have great respect for the women out there who are doing what they need to do to get the job done also.)

By now you probably forgot all about the Fortune 400 list. I knew happiness wasn't all about the money (money only empowers you to be more of the good or bad that you are), but I knew that money was a big part of it. As a teen, it was probably the only measuring stick I had.

After seeing Mr. Smith at the grocery store it really made me think, so I broke out my copy of the Forbes 400 list of the richest Americans. Can you guess what I found? **None of them had a job.**

(Let's take a second and let that sink in.)

Yep, none of them had a job. Matter of fact, there were then, and still are, quite a few people on that list including the one at the top, who didn't even have a college education. One of them only made it to the 8th grade.

So what did I do? I went to my teacher with the list and said with sincere respect (since I figured out he was just following the path someone told him), "There are 300 million people in this country, all of them going through life the way you are teaching us students. None of them have made it on this list. If even an ounce of what you are teaching was true, someone would have lucked out and ended up here, and they haven't. I think we have been lied to."

There I was with this list of people who knew how to make money and none of them did it the way that every adult in my life was telling me to do it.

Chapter Two:

Buying the Lie

So what did all the people on the Forbes 400 list have in common? They all made their money from ownership. They owned part of the industry they made their money in and as a result, they owned their life.

News Flash: If you have a job, you don't.

Don't buy the lie of "Go to college and get a good job." Am I against college? No, not really. Well, maybe a little. But it's only because they are not teaching you what it takes to have a life of victory and achievement. It's not all their fault. Yes, there are those rare teachers who can inspire you. So don't get me wrong, but look at the whole picture.

What does that mean? Most colleges don't teach how to start and run a business beyond the cookie cutter "Business school" curriculum which is nothing more than some useful information that you could just as easily get from a good business book. A business school for the most part is a good place to find an employee. It shouldn't be that way! They should be teaching more. Teaching more about creativity, personal growth, strategic thinking, people skills, and so on, but for some reason, they are not.

Matter of fact, in most cases they (institutions of higher education) are so set up to just teach an easily duplicated model or system that they can actually inhibit your ability to think. Now, I don't mean stopping your ability to think as far as "What is that flying tin bird in the sky?" I mean original thought, person to person interaction and neurolinguistic programming. It is your ability to think and implement those thoughts that is the very life blood of success and happy living.

Think about it! Ha, no pun intended. What college put the plans for Disney World in Walt's head? What systematic teaching model inspired Larry Ellison to have his unsystematic approach to business or Richard Branson and his creative marketing he applies to his empire? The answer is none.

So why do we all (well, most of us) buy into this faulty thought process? Our education system, endless hours of television, and video game addictions are all probable contributing factors.

The most important element to success though is - **don't buy the lie.** There is nothing that is taught at the university that cannot be taught through apprenticeship or mentorship. (Finding those two things is a key to victory.)

Because people have not been able to achieve the life they thought education would provide, they have instead used the education itself as the marker of success. Matter of fact, the more they are disappointed in their lack of the real success they were after, the more they will tell you how important education is. So let me get this straight. Your education didn't provide what you thought it would, and instead of realizing that, you think the answer is more education? This train of thought floors me, but I will give you a couple examples to prove my point.

An engineer friend of my grandmother is a very smart man when it comes to education. He is very proud of this, and he won't let you forget it. Then there's my grandma; she grew up in rural America which is where her education came from.

One day, the engineer was bragging about his education and I.Q. My grandma, who didn't even graduate high school, takes an I.Q. test at his request to prove *his* intelligence. Guess what happened next? You guessed it! My grandma's score was higher than the engineer's. Oh, was he upset for WEEKS. His main rebuttal, "Well, I'm an engineer, you couldn't be an engineer. My education is more in depth than what is found on a simple I.Q. test." To finish painting this picture about education not equaling success, in the 40's or 50's he found oil. Don't get too excited. He said that getting the oil, hiring staff, and investing time for something so risky wouldn't be a smart move. He re-enforced his belief that he should stay away from this endeavor because it would have been in a subject matter that was outside that of which he was educated in (notice how people limit their endeavors to their educational false floor). Today, he lives in an 8-plex apartment building, and the oil field was recently profiled on national news as the largest oil announcement in the last 50 years.

Want another one?

I had a meeting with a young lady who I was considering for a position in one of my companies. She was going to a very nice, very private school. She was spending $120,000 for her education, and this was back in 2000. I was shocked and curious. What kind of career path did this girl want to pursue that would put her six figures in debt by the time she's 21 years old? Her answer? A flight attendant. Don't laugh, she is a nice lady. Ok, I chuckled too. Don't feel bad. I asked her, "Do you know you don't have to have a college degree to perform and excel in that position?" Her reply was, "I know, but if I do, I will make $4,000 per year more than without it." Which of course my reply was "What? You will go over $120,000 + interest in debt to make $1.92 more per hour? At that rate, it will take you 60 years to make what you spent!" Obviously, this lady did not get the position. How could I in good conscious hire a lady who couldn't do basic math?

Now, don't write in to tell me that her college degree will lead to promotions faster. That would still mean she's working for someone else. Besides, that's not really true. Promotions are based on mostly ability, and if the company thinks education is THAT important for some reason, they will educate her. A successful company knows that what makes a stand out employee is never their education.

Okay, one more story, that's it.

A billionaire was having a discussion with someone I know. At the same time frame there was this guy (I think his name was Jennings) setting a record on the popular TV show, Jeopardy. So the guy I know asks this billionaire, "How much would you pay a guy that smart to be on your staff?" Obviously, he was expecting some outrageous number, mid to high six figures at least. The billionaire's answer? "About $165." To which this man replied "$165,000 is kind of low, don't you think?" The billionaire responds, "No, not $165,000. I mean just $165. That's about what it costs for a good set of encyclopedias."

The billionaire knew what I am telling you. Education means pretty much nothing in the *bigger picture* of living the life you were meant to have, which is the whole point of this book.

I realize this can be a painful chapter. You spent a good portion of your life and a lot of money getting your education, but the fact that you even read chapter one shows that you want more depth, more meaning, and more adventure than what you are having now. The "now" you have is based on what you know, how you think and what actions you take.

I am glad you have your education; a person should never stop learning. I just want to point out that when it comes to victory and achievement, we have all been lied to. Don't kill the messenger.

Another lie that floors me is the statistic that the average college graduate makes more in their lifetime than a high school graduate (on average, of course). But what they don't tell you is that the college graduate starts out more in debt than the high school graduate, which means the high school graduate has a leg up from the beginning. Yeah, never thought about that did you? Let me guess, people in your life also tell you that it is better to buy a home and have a mortgage than it is to rent because you build equity, right? RUN AWAY FROM THEM!

In an article "The Case Against the College Degree" for *Smart Money,* author Jack Hough tells the story of two young men Ernie and Bill:

> "Bill has a typical college experience. He gets into a public college and after two years transfers to a private one. He spends $49,286 on tuition and required fees, the average for such a track. I'm not counting room and board, since Bill must pay for his keep whether he goes to college or not. Bill gets average-size grants, adjusted for average probabilities of receiving them, and so pays $34,044 for college. He leaves school with an average-size loan and a good interest rate: $17,450 at 5%. The $16,594 he has saved for college, you see, is precisely enough to pay what his loans don't cover.
>
> Bill will have higher pay than Ernie his whole life, starting at $23,505 after taxes and peaking at $56,808. Like Ernie, he sets aside 5%. At that rate, it will take him 12 years to pay off his loan. Debt-free at 34, he starts adding to the same index fund as Ernie, making bigger monthly contributions with his higher pay. But when the two reunite at 65 for a retirement party, Ernie will have grown his savings to nearly $1.3 million. Bill will have less than a third of that."

Then there is the book "Going Broke by Degree" Economics professor Richard Vedder points out that after 6 years in a bachelor's program 40% of all students will not have a degree, but will still have six years of college debt to pay.

Two more things when it comes to financial success and how it relates to education. Ever hear the saying "In the game of life 'A' students work for 'B' students, who in turn are managed by 'C' students and the 'D' students owns the company"? It's truer than what they are telling you.

While your boss (who never sees his kids and is on wife #3) may require that you have a B.S. to get that extra $2.00/hr, business investors and banks never ask for a report card! Not the good ones anyway.

Chapter Three:

I Don't *Necessarily* Hate Your Boss

When reading this book, it would be very easy to come to the conclusion that I am anti-job. Well, yes and no. While I do not want anyone to have a job, you need one at times until you can break free. In a way, you cannot experience freedom if you have not experienced captivity.

That being said, I appreciate jobs as well. I want someone to wash my cars, and someone to take book orders; but I want each of the people who work for me to be replaced as they move on to live the life of their dreams. I doubt they want the highlight of their life to be working for me.

When you are working for a powerful company, big or small (some of the most powerful companies are small) you can be part of a ship that goes against the tide and can have an impact on your community, state, country and even the world. I don't know how I want to do this yet, but somehow on my website I would like to let the world of 6+ billion people know which companies are worth working "with" and those whose products and employment should be avoided like the plague.

Notice I said working "WITH". While you are an employee get it out of your head that you are working "FOR" that company. Slavery is dead in this country. If your boss stopped paying you, you would stop showing up. It's a mutually agreed upon situation. While I admit that most of you should get a different job, or better yet, no job, it is still your choice to work where you do.

So what should you look for in a business that will work as an employer until you are freed from employment all together?

A very important thing to look for is a company that takes a stand. I want you to take a stand when you have your own business. Why expect less from your employer?

In addition to a company that takes a stand on important issues, other things I would look for in a place to work would be:

- A company that provides income sufficient enough for you to start using that money in your game plan to escape.

- Co-workers that do not become a drain on you emotionally or cause you to engage in actions that go against your moral beliefs.

- A boss who understands that you are not going to be there forever and encourages you to move on and become the best you can be.

- A job that just gets it done. By that I mean, while you may be attracted to having a job that challenges you intellectually or has a certain amount of status don't take it. Take the job where you can get money, but also does not drain your energy or require 50-60 hours a week. Your plan is to get out in less than two years I'm assuming, so just use the job for what it can offer you to escape.

While employment for you is temporary, giving your best effort is still important. Don't be a slacker because if you are when it comes to your job it will create in you a habit to be a slacker in all areas of your life. Do a good job; make the boss sorry to see you leave. You never know, you just might take your boss with you when you go.

Chapter Four:

Yes, It Is As Bad As You Think It Is.

Now that we have praised the bosses of the world I want to use the next few pages to bring us back to reality for a minute by reminding you why you need to quit your job or die.

Remember how I was saying that your employment was your choice, and you are not a slave? While that is very true, please, don't get the impression that you are free either.

Free is being able to do what you want to do, when you want to do it. As I will point out shortly, you are so far from free it's not even funny.

Before I tell you the bad news, let me give you a suggestion. Kind of like a spoonful of sugar helping the medicine go down. There is a great book on how to live while you are in prison (prison = your job) while you are planning your escape. It's called "The Four Hour Work Week" by Tim Ferris. Keeping with the prison theme, he explains how to make the cook bring you cigarettes and how to talk the warden into walking his dog. It's a very good book by a man who has escaped from his prison. So go pick up a copy, after you read the rest of this book, of course.

So how bad is a job and why do I call it a prison? Let's have you decide. While some of my reader's prisons may be "minimum security" others will have maximum security, and I'm sure you will see the reality of your prison in your life through these examples.

Prison	**Jobs**
Can't have personal calls	Can't have personal calls
Have pre-approved dress code	Have pre-approved dress code
Can't pick your cell mates	Can't pick your co-workers
Can't move out	Where you live and the home you have is restricted by your paycheck

Food options suck	Food options restricted by your paycheck
No women	While you MAY BE able to get one, your prison sentence (job) will cause disaster.
Woken up when you would rather sleep every morning	"BEEP, BEEP, BEEP" Sound familiar?
No vacation plan	Vacation time and activity restricted by your paycheck
Find yourself staring out the window	Find yourself staring out the window
To succeed you must lower your standards	To succeed you must lower your standards
Free healthcare, cable, gym membership	They make you pay for these things
Gain freedom in 40 years	Gain freedom in 40+ years

Isn't it sad to think that what kind of car you have, where you live, what your furniture looks like, and what school your kids go to is all decided by everyone but you?

~~

Relationships are a very important part of a happy life, so how does a job affect a relationship?

Wow, let me count the ways. A hero of mine, Bradley, pointed out to me what I'm about to point out to you. This is probably some of the most powerful, poignant, and on the mark business and life teaching I have ever heard. One of the many things I have learned from Bradley has to do with that very tough question. How does a job affect your relationships?

A man and a woman decide to get married. First, that man should hit his knees and thank God for her because she can do much better. Then he should ask for the strength to be a good husband. Men—, and I'm talking to the men because I am one. Men, when you stood in front of a pastor, priest, judge or ship's captain, your wife put her whole life, her WHOLE life in your hands. Don't treat it lightly. Her hopes, dreams, fears, and desires are all your responsibility. She loves you (for some unknown

32

reason) and you should want to love her, cherish her and adore her. If this does not register with you and you are married, do your marriage a favor and look up Tim and Gaye Goad at www.timgoad.com. They have some great marriage resources.

One of the first things Tim and Gaye ask couples they counsel is what is their shared vision for the future? What is their common goal, what are they working *together* to achieve?

I know you may be thinking that's a little off topic, but if you don't know what you are working for or what is really important, you are in a worse position than you think.

Anyway, everyday a married couple wakes up and the wife gets on her prettiest clothes, spends 45 minutes putting on her make-up, doing her hair, and putting on that pretty smelling perfume. She then spends 40-60 hours a week away from her husband, trying to impress the other men in her life. Usually, her boss is a male; she tries her hardest to impress him, and give him her best all day, every day. He gets her respect, her adoration and her time, and she gets the same from him, every day. Then she comes home, puts on that old pair of sweat pants and old shirt, lets her hair down and washes off that make-up. She is exhausted from her hard day. When she does see her husband which is usually only 15 min before bed due to kids, phone calls and paying bills, she gives him her exhausted, stressed out and grouchy parts of her life. Yeah, that has love life written all over it.

Then, on the husband's side: He goes to work and pursues a goal (important to men) without his wife. Usually with the help of a female co-worker, who just like his wife, is trying to impress the men her life. Ever hear of an affair happening at work? Usually it has an excuse like "she understands me, cares about what I care about". Well, why wouldn't she? She gets to see him pursue a dream—his wife doesn't. She gets to see him step up and be a man; his wife thinks he's a lazy, unromantic bum.

Not only does a job cause the above, but when you look at the top three reasons for divorce, according to multiple counselors, they are:

1) Communication

2) Sex

3) Money

I know that's what people say but in reality it is:

1) Money

2) Money

3) Money

Here's how I get there.

Communication- If you only see each other for an hour a day of alone time, emotional separation is going to happen. Not intentionally—but the two of them are essentially leading separate lives. Have you ever heard of a couple who, once the kids leave the home, have marriage problems because they feel like they don't even know each other anymore?

Sex- When a woman doesn't respect and adore her man, she isn't going to want to have sex with him. When she has to work to the point of exhaustion because the man isn't bringing home the bacon and money isn't abundant, she is not going to have an easy time respecting him. It has nothing really to do with sexual techniques or any of those other sex issues you read about in Cosmo. Those things can be cured with practice. Practice you won't be getting, because she doesn't respect you.

Money- Do you ever notice how it is never too much of it that causes an argument?

Just think—to have a great marriage, all you have to do is quit your job.

Chapter Five:

In the Land of Pharaohs

Roy wakes up at 5:45 a.m., kisses his beautiful wife on the forehead, walks to the kitchen, and pours the 1 millionth cup of coffee. He walks out the door to get into his 7 year old car (that works most of the time) and heads to work. Roy, you see, is in one of those pyramid scheme businessmen.

He is one of the entry level workers at a large manufacturing plant, just one of a 1000 foundational employees working the floor.

Floor employees are overseen by fifty department heads; those department heads are overseen by twenty foremen. Those twenty foremen are overseen by three operations managers, and those three operational managers are overseen by two vice presidents, who in turn are ultimately overseen by the owner of the company.

When Roy's bosses, the fifty department leaders, get paid they are making their money off of Roy. If Roy doesn't do all the actual product producing work, no money would be coming into the company, so Roy works HARD. He leaves his wife, family and castle 40+ hours a week; meanwhile, Roy's boss is just making money off of Roy. It's always the guy on top of the pyramid who makes the money.

Now, Roy's boss' boss isn't only making money on Roy's boss, but also on Roy himself. Roy's boss' boss' boss is making money on Roy, Roy's boss and Roy's boss' boss, and of course, Roy himself.

So let me get this straight. Roy is at a company where all the rich people at the top of this pyramid are making money off of him? But that can't be right. Pyramids are those late night infomercial business scams, right? Let's keep examining it.

In order for Roy to move up the chain, someone else has to either get promoted, get fired, quit or die. He (Roy) doesn't really have any control over it. Yeah, he has his MBA. Yeah, he is a nice guy, but he is in the lottery of luck among his 1000 other co-workers. Sure, he can work harder, smile more, and stay late in hopes of catching the boss' attention at the expense of his own life and his family. But any of us who have had a job for longer than a week know that 80% of getting ahead in the pyramid is based on the boss' personality, goals and mood.

"But, Josh," you say "if the business expands, then Roy could have room for advancement." True, so let's look at your best case scenario.

Business at Roy's company is booming. Matter of fact, they are now going to need to add fifty new positions resulting in a flier in the break room.

"Team: Make $100 extra for every referral that becomes a new hire."

Inspired by the company's recruitment payoff, Roy gets a great idea to invite his brother over tonight for a BBQ. Roy's brother comes over for dinner totally unaware of the ulterior motive. Sitting there at the patio table, Roy starts telling his brother about this opportunity with the company he's working with. The factory is great, the money is good, and he can work with his brother. The next night, Roy heads to the softball field; before the game and between innings Roy is telling his buddies how they should get involved with the company. "Guys, just come down to the company and check it out. They are having an open house and one of the VP's is going to be giving a talk about the future of manufacturing. How can you say no to something you haven't really checked out yet?"

Let's carry this out even further.

Roy is a success. He and his wife are both really excited about the extra $600 they are getting from Roy recruiting others to join him in the company. Roy's boss is impressed and decides to promote him. The boss puts these six new employees under Roy. This means Roy has to do less work and gets to make more money off of his friend's hard work.

Wow, making money off of other people? Getting paid to talk your family and friends into joining up? That sounds just like a... well, let's not say yet. Let's keep up our examination.

This wouldn't be so bad, right? What if one day Roy gets to the top of this pyramid? I mean company. So Roy spends 35 years at the factory. We know already at this point in the book Roy's marriage has a 60%+ chance of failure, his kids don't know him and are probably experimenting with drugs. Because he was working for someone else we also know he has no control financially, aging way too fast, and thinks to himself, "I wish I would have..."

Not only that, but now, every time Roy goes to his softball games his friends are saying, "Oh crap, here comes Roy. He's going to try to get us into his thing at the factory."

Then one day it happens. This is the day he has been working, recruiting and sacrificing for— the day of the big pay off. The owner of the company is going to be retiring, and today, he will be announcing who he is going to appoint as the new CEO. While Roy knows that getting this position will not give him the same privileges that the owner enjoyed; he will, however, finally be at the top of the pyramid and making money on all those 1000's below him. So, here's the big moment. Roy's wife has come to join him and everyone is gathered in the break room as the owner steps up to the make shift podium.

Boss: *"Thank you, ladies and gentlemen. It has been a pleasure over the years to be the owner of such a great company. It is you, those who work so hard every day that make this place run. Give yourself a hand.* (This is almost psychotic. He makes money off of them, tells them he used them for years, and they are too stupid to notice) *Today, I will be appointing the person who will be replacing me at the helm of this mighty ship."*

Roy sits up in his seat, and thinks to himself, "This has to be it." He's the most senior employee. His mouth gets dry, what will his first address to the staff be?

Boss: *"Ladies and gentlemen, the new CEO of xyz industries, Sean Peterson, my son, the apple of my eye. Come up here, son, I'm so proud of you."*

What? Roy is crushed. Sean has never even worked here. He's never even interned. How is this possible? Roy finds his hands clapping, but he cannot seem to hear the noise.

The next Monday, Roy has an e-mail. It's from Sean Peterson; he wants to see Roy first thing this morning.

(Wait, wait a second, readers. What are you thinking? You already know what's about to happen? Wow, I'm glad *you* don't have jobs. Anyone who knows how these stories end is smart enough to recognize that they are in the same situation. However, for those who don't know yet, let's keep going.)

Sean: *"Roy, come in, come in. Roy you have served us well and we appreciate you* (making me a millionaire). *However Roy, I need to do some restructuring and will have to be letting you go. Please though, take the week to get your stuff packed up. We don't want you out today, were not slave drivers after all."*

This story plays out thousands of times a day, and if you get a paycheck, you ARE part of it. I know that most of you never thought you were in a pyramid scheme but you are. Don't try to argue, it's a fact.

I put this chapter in here because I have seen on my own when talking to someone about starting their own business they say, "Oh, this sounds like one of those pyramid things, that's not for me." Someday, I know someone will come to you with some form of business

45

opportunity, a way out of your prison cell, and when that day comes I don't want you to look stupid. While I admit that not all business offers are legit, a lot of them are and you would be wise to find a way out of your prison.

Just for fun, let's look at some jobs/industries that are multi-level or "Pyramid" businesses that you may not have thought about.

- Retail (Target, Wal-Mart)
- Law
- Health Care
- Construction
- Utilities
- Banking and Finance
- Communications
- Service and Hospitality
- Government (BIG SCAM JOBS)
- Real Estate
- Television, Radio and Media
- Manufacturing
- Politics

Believe me when I say that this list is just the tip, of the tip, of the iceberg. Unless YOU own it, it owns you, or at least rents you and your body for the purpose of the labor your body and mind can be bought for.

In America, we call someone who rents themselves out for the use of another a prostitute. I'm just sayin'. Now, that is a little harsh and if you don't know, I used the term "prostitute" for 49% comedic emphasis.

The fact that pyramids exist is not a bad thing in and of itself. The bad thing is being stupid and denying you are in them. While all jobs are pyramids (see "I don't necessarily hate your boss" chapter) there are some good ones.

Church: 1 pastor, 2-3 jr. pastors, 7 deacons, 10 group leaders and 500 congregates.

Military: General, hand full of Majors, 100's of lieutenants, and millions of soldiers.

The funny thing is that while you operate in pyramids in many areas of your life, making money is the easiest way to get out of them.

Chapter Six:

The Coming Storm

I have never been in Florida the days before a hurricane comes ashore. I can imagine it though. The waves start to come in a little stronger and the gentle breeze begins to ring the wind chimes outside the kitchen window. The next day you wake up and the waves are now crashing against the shore. On your way to work, you drive along the coast and the sea spray from those waves now makes its way across your windshield. The weatherman on the radio is talking about how warm water is building this behemoth of a hurricane. You arrive at work, and everyone is now a meteorologist. The office is a buzz about the hurricane, and some of the older people are telling stories about the last "big one."

Your drive home gives you a very odd feeling down in your stomach. It's a mix of anxiety, fear and excitement of the moment. You can almost taste the chemical makeup of emotion in your mouth as you look out your windshield and way off in the distance you can see the dark clouds at the edge of the horizon.

When you get to your home, you and your spouse head to the hardware store to buy plywood, food, candles, batteries, and duct tape.

Just like you, there are thousands of your neighbors in line at those places with you. Everyone knows what's coming, and they know they must be ready. Gone is the empty conversation at the checkout about Jessica Simpson on the cover of a magazine or the stop at the hot dog stand on the way out. Everyone is talking about something they cannot prevent.

Knowing what to do to prepare makes the fear more tolerable.

Once you get your windows boarded up, and the back screen door duct taped shut with a 2x4 across it as added support; you and your spouse take a cup of coffee and sit in the front porch swing, wrapped up in a blanket together.

The sun is getting lower in the sky, and the once very distance gray clouds now look to be a stone's throw from the shore. You can see the distant lightning flashes and the deep, loud rumble of the thunder raises the hair on the back of your neck.

The feeling that was once noticeable but soft on your way home from work has now become a knot in your stomach. The weatherman says that they are shutting down the city; no non-official travel should be conducted.

The day grows dark, bringing night hours early. Not because the sun has sped up its descent, but because this monstrous storm has defeated the beautiful sun. As the darkness encompasses you and your spouse, you notice the street lights come to life hours before normal. Your knot has now moved to your throat (even as you read this your heart is pounding faster than before and you now feel this fear.)

The coffee is now gone. You know what comes next; hide for your life! You realize your porch swing must come down so you release if from its anchor above. This gentle piece of furniture that just brought you joy will soon become deadly. You walk toward your door, and you turn one last time to say a small prayer as you realize some of those standing in line with you earlier may not be living in the morning. Lightning destroys your moment of reflection as the storm now seems to be screaming your name.

You enter your home, the shelter you hope you sufficiently prepared to keep your demise at bay. Just as your front door shuts, at that very moment that was not one second too late, your door meets the storm head on. As this beast unleashes the demons against your shelter, the rain pounds and the winds howl. You look out an open crack in your window and while just a moment ago the outside world was so dark, it now is trumped by the blackness of your hiding place. The power is out, and the dark gray outside seems bright compared to your dark enclave.

Powerless, you sneak another peek out of your boarded up window. There, in the darkness is a police car. It's red and blue lights break up the darkness in flashes. The cop is out there because what once seemed unimaginable is now a reality. Out in this relentless storm there are people who didn't heed the warnings. Stupidity or ignorance, the difference doesn't matter as to the reason of their fate. A tear falls down the cheek of your wife, out of sympathy for the lost souls who don't stand a chance.

How does this relate to you, your family and your financial choices?

Let's see how well you recognize the signs of a coming storm.

- Oil was at an all time high, going from $8 a barrel in the early 1980's to over $137 by June, 2008 which is a 1,600% increase. Your wage went up that much to compensate, didn't it? Then down to below $35 in February 2009, but gas prices at the pump did not recede to reflect the change.
- The dollar and the world economy it affects are at near record lows.
- Approval of both political parties is at all time lows.
- Airlines are taking out ovens, phones, and seats to reduce the weight of the plane to save fuel.
- Gigantic mortgage collapse.
- Companies lay off tens of thousands of people at a time.
- Out sourcing. Have you heard of it?
- National debt is at an all time high and almost unsolvable levels.

- If you are under the age of 65 you may as well not count on Social Security.
- School shootings are now common place.
- Bankruptcy is soaring.
- Divorces are 60% or higher.
- The amount of money Americans put into savings is actually LESS than zero.
- Teen suicide and depression are epidemic.
- The "Bail Outs" of 2009 will put your great grandchildren in debt.

I could go on and on, but you get the point. Just like with an approaching hurricane, you can tell what's coming, so too is it with the storm that is about to hit the global economy and your family directly.

When even billionaires are making preparations for a coming storm, do not for one second think your "good" $300k a year job will withstand the winds of chaos which is about to blow down on you. If you make less than that, you should already be reading this book for a second time. You are like a resident of Kansas who lives in a trailer park, and you don't even have a basement to hide in.

Today, as I write this there was a story on cable news about how money is so tight, and the state of the economy so bad that they are washing airplanes more often as it saves 1.5% in fuel costs. Less dirt, less drag, less fuel use...

Come on people! A weatherman can only interrupt your favorite show so many times before it's too late. To put it another way, it's like you are waking up on the Titanic and seeing the crew bailing water. How long would it take you to figure out staying in your room may be the wrong move to make?

Want another example? The price for the amount of wheat that went in a loaf of bread six months before I wrote this sentence was 10 cents. Now, it's 40 cents. For those who are not good at math, that is *not* a 30% increase. I mean if it were a 30% increase that would be terrible. World crisis terrible. Can you imagine a 30% increase in a six month time frame? If you didn't get a 30% increase in your wage in that same time period at work you should literally walk out the door because you job is actually causing you to go suffer.

Whew, so now that we know it's not a 30% increase what percentage increase is it? Well let's see, two...carry the zero, no it can't be. Oh my gosh, are you sitting down? It's an increase of 300%. Let me spell that out so you don't think I accidentally added a zero. That is a three hundred percent increase!

Wake up. This is no joke. The fact that the world is facing a hard time is real. It's here, and if you think you can just stay where you are and do nothing, you are like a man fishing in a rowboat as a hurricane hits.

I know you may be thinking that it's just a mild recession. A 300% increase in wheat is NOT a recession! The worse part is its not going to get better for most people for a very long time.

Read Harry S. Dent's book "The Next Great Bubble Boom", it serves as just one example of what you may have been ignoring. Suffice it to say, fifteen years from now will possibly be so bad that it will make the great depression look like a 24 hour flu bug.

Let me make this clear as it's very, VERY important. If you make $50,000 and receive let's say a 5% cost of living increase, you are making an extra $2,500. After taxes you are making approximately $1,700 more than last year. Now if the cost of your life went up 30% (which is an understatement) then your life actually went backward 25%. What happens in 4 years? Do the math.

Chapter Seven:

Hope Is Not Lost For Those Who Quit Their Job

Ally hope is not lost, however. You can survive the storm, and if you act as soon as you finish this book, you can actually thrive. That's right, THRIVE.

During tough financial times for an economy, windows of great opportunity open, and if you are in a position to take advantage of it you can create massive amounts of wealth for you, your children and even your great grandchildren.

However, if you have any of the following, it will greatly hinder that ability if not eliminate you from it all together:

- Debt
- Mortgage (yes, I know that's debt, do you?)
- A Job
- A portfolio of only stock

Just as one example, let's use the Baby Boomers (The generation of people born from 1946-1964). They make up the largest age demographic in America, and they will all be entering retirement over the next 15 years. Most of them have the majority of their net worth tied up in a home with an existing mortgage. In some cases, people have a second, third or even worse, a reverse mortgage.

So, let's say we are 15 years in the future. What happens when 100 million people want to sell their homes and there are only 7 million people willing to buy? Prices fall faster than attendance at a Ben Affleck movie. Not to mention most will be sold for less than what they owe, creating a seller who is still in debt after the sale of an asset, or a "negative value factor". This means that the baby boomers will be liquid asset deficient, which means they will not be putting money into the economy. Not to mention the Social Security factor of more people collecting than paying in.

In this negative situation, builders will not be building, meaning employees will be laid off at building supply stores, which will trickle down to the paint manufacturers who have to lay off employees, so on and so forth. This effect will continue to snowball into all industries.

Just like when there are more home sellers than buyers the prices go down; the same holds true for jobs.

When you have 1 million jobs and 25 million people (less than 10% of the population) needing work, what happens?

Chaos is a good answer.

This example is not even considering other factors like inflation, continued increased costs for fuel and food, a weakening dollar, national debt increase, poor Presidential administrations and heaven forbid, another terrorist attack.

"But, Josh, isn't this chapter a chapter of hope?" Well, of course. Let's say that your family was smart and did not listen to the way of fools or followed the masses to demise. You took some wise counsel from men and women who have lived a life of significance and invested time in your family's dreams, in your children's lives instead of your boss'. As your cash money situation grew, your debt shrank and by the time the economy gets really bad, you are debt free (including your mortgage) and have money to spare.

So you wake up and say to your wife "My love, have I ever told you I want to own a mansion?" Sure enough, after looking on-line you find a wonderful home, 7,500 square feet, right on the coast a pool, guest quarters and a 6 car garage. Taking a look at this home it sold for $7,000,000 when the current owner bought it. You ask what he is asking, and when you hear the answer your heart starts to beat faster. The price is $900,000. Better yet, the seller lost all of his money and the house is now on auction for $250,000 in back taxes. Don't believe this will happen? It already is!

So over the next few years you decide you like real estate and pick up 10 other homes for $250,000 each. You also purchase a cattle ranch that used to do $12,000,000 in business for the bargain price of $1 million. Not to mention you finally got that red Ferrari that company executive had to sell to pay off his debt and that Arabian pony you bought for your 8 yr old daughter was what the buyer called a "bleeding expense." The world now becomes your playground and your church or other charity outreaches are blessed in times when their counterparts are in desperation.

Ready for the real magic? The economy makes a comeback, either from Americans regaining the American dream or from foreign influence using our economy for what it was designed for. (Wealth can be in any government, any economy, and any situation).

Your 10 homes that you bought for a total of $2.5 million are now all back over $3 million each. Not their original value but way above what you paid for them, making you a nice $27.5 million profit. Remember, you do not need a good economy to make money! You also have your cattle ranch back making its $12 million a year. Don't forget, the world still eats beef.

But what if I'm wrong? What if you start your own business, start owning your own life and the economy doesn't get bad at all? If you are asking that question, you do not understand and you are missing the whole point of the book. Don't worry; I forgive you, just keep reading.

Chapter Eight:

You're Worth More than This

Sitting in a hotel lobby, I was waiting for my next appointment. It is a beautiful hotel, with a multistory water fall in the ten story tall atrium. Behind the water fall, a glass elevator was making its way up and down, carrying guests to and fro.

My appointment was running late and my cranberry juice was nearing the bottom of the glass. The man I was meeting had convinced me that it was worth my time to meet with him. I myself was not so sure, he seemed mildly cocky. You know the type, drives a Lexus (leased) has a nice home (mortgaged) and his professional wife (well, not a professional WIFE, but a wife who had a profession).

Anyway, he finally arrives—late—and treats me with a smug "Hello". Evidently, this man was thinking it was I who was lucky enough to meet with him. My, the naive are fun sometimes.

He sits down and with "that" kind of attitude says "Ok, so what do you got?" So I say, "Let's slow down a second, Bubba. I think we are off on the wrong impression. It's not what I have that we need to evaluate, it's I who needs to decide if YOU are worth me finishing my cranberry juice here or in my car on the way home."

You see, he did make a higher income than I (at the time) and due to his lack of logic and reason, he assumed that he was the one with something to offer me that I needed. His reply was exposing.

"I already make a good living so I'm probably not interested," he quipped.

That was it, I had enough. The one thing I cannot stand is people who don't think, who don't evaluate, who don't reason.

"You are right," I said. "You work hard for your $250,000 a year (I purposely over stated what he made) and if you THINK that puts you in a good position, than I truly feel sorry for you. And due to the lack of actual thought you put into your life, I probably couldn't work with you anyway. I'm not a good babysitter."

He huffed and puffed, and I used a communication technique that I developed to keep him sitting down as I continued. Then I said, "I do have a question though, just out of curiosity. You have a wife, and I'm sure she is lovely. How much is she worth to you?"

He, of course, said that she is priceless to which I said "If she is priceless to you, why do you sell her for $40 an hour to her boss?" Harsh? Yes, I know, but he had the audacity to get cocky because he used his current situation against my then situation as a foundation for evaluation. He needed to be knocked down to reality. How does the song go? "You got to be cruel to be kind", in the right measure, of course.

So what's my point with this entertaining little story?

A couple of things. One, he didn't make $250,000 per year; it was more like $80k. In addition, his wife didn't work for $40/hr; it was more like $15. So why did I use a number I knew was larger than reality when talking to him? That is a key training point, which I will not take the time here to teach.

Part of the reason is, it calmed him down, and humbled him enough to make him realize he is not anywhere near where he thought he was. Yes, it hurt him, but I had to do it out of love. Do you know what happened next?

This is where we learn from his example, so we don't have to do it the hard way.

His pride kept him from realizing what his wife was really worth. There is no way you could buy my time with my wife from me. I don't want to get to the end of my life and wish I could have spent more lunches with her, more travel with her, more old movies and popcorn on a late night with her.

Think about this. Let's say your wife makes $30,000 a year. After taxes and expenses, it's under $20k take home, less than $2,000 per month, a lousy $2k. I know that money is tight and it could mean shoes for the kids. If you think my teaching here is belittling to you, you are 100% wrong. I am from a place where $50 would change my month, and I have the utmost respect for your family doing what you have to do to make it!

My point is, you don't just have to make it. The reason you are in the position you are in is because you have a job. I know you are worth much more than that.

I know this is going to be painful but keep in mind, I was where you are. I don't want to hurt you, but get you to move. The reason it is uncomfortable to read these things is because deep down in your heart, there is a small ember that still knows you can achieve something great in your life. As you read this book, the amber starts to burn as your dream is fueled with hope and possibility. The pain you are feeling is actually the hardened casing around your heart that has been restricting your life beginning to release its grip.

With that in mind, and knowing that it is never too late to have a great life, let's talk about your children.

I know you would give your life for your children. You do give it actually by going to work every day. Why are your boss' kids worthy of a private education and your kids are not? Your boss' kids are going to that private school, getting a great education to make their future bright while it's being paid for by YOUR efforts. So why aren't your kids going to private school on your efforts?

Your priceless wife, who works way too hard whether at home or at a job, would love to take a 14 day cruise where she can be treated and pampered like a queen. You paid for your boss' wife to go because of your hard work. Why not your own wife?

The world economy is not a pie where there is only so much to go around. In the book *Unlimited Wealth*, by Paul Zane Pilzer, he explains in simple terms how there is more than enough for everyone to be wealthy. It's not a limited amount of wealth which you either have or don't have. Knowing this, the only reason...THE ONLY REASON you are not wealthy is the person who looks back at you in the mirror!

Chapter Nine:

Dave Ramsey, HELP!

D
ebt is a beast that shows no mercy. Those who have had to deal with debt know it's a cancer to living a happy life. How big is this beast? Well, before we get to a personal level, let's just take a look at our national debt.

The national debt by the government of the United States of America is $9,395,782,929,009.98 or to make is simple, $9.4 TRILLION dollars. Since September 28, 2007 it has been growing at the rate of $1.57 billion dollars PER DAY! That's a hungry beast.

*Update note: The above number is before the $1.2 trillion stimulus package passed by President Obama.

According to the Department of Debt, in 1929 America was $16 billion dollars in debt (look at what happened in American economic history in 1913.) As of FY 2007, it broke the $9 TRILLION mark. That's 563 times bigger or 56,300% growth! Fifty-six <u>thousand</u> percent. Not including our own personal debt, it would take $30,000 from each American man, woman and child to pay it off. What's really crazy is that half of that debt has been since 1990. Now if you add in personal, business, trust fund, state and local debt, collectively we are $53,000,000,000,000,000.00 in debt. So every man, woman and child has to pony up $175,000.

As far as America's governmental debt, the economy, illegal tax codes and the lie behind taxes in the first place, I will cover all that in another book. I just wanted to point out that the country we live in is going down faster than a lead balloon and unless more people become self-employed, your children's great-great grandchildren will still be paying off what our grandparents did.

Credit Cards:

Reach into your wallet or purse. Do you see any credit cards? Odds are you have more than one. Odds are you are also losing money on that card. Yes, even if you have no credit card debt and pay off the bill on time, it can still cost you money. For example, (I don't know if they have changed it) just one card, the GE Rewards card would penalize those who pay off their bill on time. Granted it was only $25 per year, but it's the whole principal of the thing. Did you know 75% of all card revenue comes from finance charges?

For the rest of you, the "average" American, you carry $8,500 in credit card debt. I know an average is an average, but don't be ignorant. When most people who don't have credit card debt or worse yet, financial advisors, spout the fact that "Only 8.3% of Americans have *more* than $8,500 in credit card debt." They tend to think that as long as it's not them, it doesn't affect them. How immature and silly. That would be like saying, "I ride a bike so the cost of fuel going up doesn't affect me". Then you go and buy dinner which is up 40% in the past 3 months because of fuel costs.

What I'm saying is, make sure you see the bigger picture, outside the world of your "expertise" before you believe stupid things.

Overdraft fees:

An overdraft fee is when the bank charges a fee to cover a debit request on your account when you do not have the funds to cover the transaction with your deposited funds.

I realize that most of you who are reading this are not regularly subject to these fees, but just like the credit card issues, listen up, as it does affect you.

According to a news article in Newsday citing FDIC stats, overdraft fee totals are around $23.7 billion annually and growing. The amount the average account is "shy" when the overdraft fee is placed on the account is less than the fee itself. Meaning more money is profited by the banks than the temporary deficiencies. When the deficiency is taken care of with a deposit, the overdraft fee becomes a HUGE profit point for the bank.

How does this affect you if you do not have overdraft problems? Well, if your customer base for your business or your boss' business is $23.7 billion dollars lighter than they needed to be, you are not going to be selling as much of whatever product or service you offer.

As for the banks, you have to watch out for these lying snakes. They can be worse than used car salesmen. The real morally bankrupt among them do things like process all debits for the day before they process all deposits and credits for the day. I have personally had this happen to me in the past. I deposited $700, but because they processed all debits first at the close of the day, I was $2 short in my account, making all debits that day, insufficiently funded. They then charged me $300 in over draft fees, leaving me with $400 in liquid cash instead of the $698 I would have had if they operated with a level of maturity.

My advice, avoid banks with irresponsible operating practices like this. Even if you are wealthy, go someplace that values economic growth. Remember, when they processed my debits before my credits, that was $300 I couldn't spend in your restaurant, movie theater or business opportunity.

Just to stop some ignorant banker from saying something stupid like, "But those fees still go into the local economy, just not through you." NO, NO, NO. Fees are pure profit, and with banks having a lot of overseas (increasingly Arab) ownership, that lost money went bye-bye to an investment that will probably be counter productive to me, you and the objecting banker.

Pay Day Loans:

These are popping up across America. I admit, part of what makes me an expert is experience in this industry as well. Matter of fact, I even signed a petition once to keep these places open. My bad. I am a real man, which means I admit when I'm wrong. I was wrong.

These companies charge a staggering 900% interest or more. Do NOT go to any of these places! I'm writing this to the single mom who needs milk money, and the college kid who needs to fix his car. I know it can be tempting when you are bleeding anything looks like a bandage, but don't do it.

It can create a constant down fall that can take years, if ever, to get out of. Putting you further into a bad life than you would be if you would have found another option.

Auto Debt:

Did you know that most millionaires buy used cars? Did you know that most new cars are sold to people who are already in debt and cannot pay cash for the new car, so they just add on more debt? This is just keeping their family from living in a mansion, traveling the world, and developing close relationships. I know, just hold on, I will make it all make sense in a minute.

When millionaires buy used cars, ask yourself, "Is it possible that they are millionaires because they do things differently?" They can afford it, but don't buy it. You can't afford it, but do buy it. It doesn't take rocket science, but I see a difference right there.

Most obviously, there is the loss of worth. You buy a car for $25,000, and four minutes after you sign the paper and the tires leave the lot it's only worth $19,500. This means even if you think you got a great rate at 0% interest you are paying a $25,000 loan for a $19,500 car. No offense, but you are stupid. The only time you should pay for a new car is when you are buying an experience, not the car itself. What do I mean? Let's say you have earned the right to buy a new car, meaning you can pay cash. Your mom has never had a new car and you want to make her dream come true. So you drive her to the car dealer and tell her to pick one. That's buying an experience. In that case, I would be willing to pay over sticker, because making dreams come true is priceless for the ones you love.

The biggest thing to remember with debt is, it takes away options. If you are managing to stay afloat with your debt and a business opportunity comes along, will you be able to go after it? Probably not. If there is a chance for your son to go to baseball camp that wasn't in your "budget" because an opening became available, can you provide him with that experience? Probably not.

It's sad to think that opportunity could knock, you could even answer, but you couldn't run after it, because your chain of debt keeps you anchored to your job.

Chapter Ten:

Becoming Superman or Wonder Woman

You walk slowly down the hall. It has been another late night at work and as you walk, you are careful with each placement of your step as not to wake anyone. You step over the creaky spot by the bathroom; you pick up the little doll your toe inconveniently found in the dimly light corridor. Why does this hallway always seem longer when you are trying to be quiet?

Finally, you reach your late night destination, and now, at a speed even slower than moments before, you open the pink door with the utmost caution.

In this room filled with dolls you don't seem to remember and tea cups you haven't pretended to drink from, you see your little princess. In her little bed with the warm glow of her "Dora" nightlight providing you just enough light to see the area around her bed and not much more, you sit down beside her. "When did she get so big?" you ask yourself as you lightly brush the hair out of her face.

Looking around the bed you see a poster of Miley Cyrus (aka Hanna Montana), and there on her night stand you see a framed school project with the trade mark red pen of a teacher "Great Job, I'm proud of you." – Mr. Smith. At the foot of her bed is the Disney Princess sleeping bag you gave her last Christmas. It's all packed up and ready for the camping trip that you can't go on. Your eyes begin to water; your heart begins to wilt.

As you sit quietly in your little girl's room, the same little girl who has her daddy's heart wrapped around her finger, you can see pictures, the signs of all the heroes in her life, and you realize that you are no longer one of them. Your mind races as you think about what it will be like when she gets older and needs her father. You probably won't be around for her first dance or her first date. Mom will probably have to teach her how to drive, but you will get to pay for the neighbor's mailbox. I guess that's something, right?

No, there are no posters in her room of you, or even many pictures of the two of you together. There are no school projects with your handwriting on them. Wincing, you know you won't be packing a sleeping bag for yourself this weekend. Matter of fact, you didn't even get to pass her the mashed potatoes at dinner tonight.

You can't take it anymore; you get up. Making your way across the room as quiet as a ninja you realize you are getting way too good at this. Whew, finally it's time for you to go to bed. When it comes to entering your room, you are quiet but not with the same amount of painstakingly thought-out caution that you used to enter your daughter's. Why not? There in your bed is a beautiful woman with moonlight dancing over her body. The body you used to ache to touch, and now, you only provide enough care to stay as silent as would be deemed respectful but far from caring. What did she do that warrants such a lack of effort from the man that once promised his life and his heart to her?

As you crawl into bed you position yourself to hold your queen, but you stop yourself. Why? Instead, rolling over the other way, your back faces hers and you close your eyes. Half asleep you turn over again. Is this a spark of passion? No, you kiss her forehead, roll back over, and say to yourself, "That's better than nothing." As you lay there, trying to calm down from your work day, you think about the last time you talked to your wife, which was fourteen long hours ago when you were leaving for work. The conversation revolved around you not being there for dinner, and you remember something about a bill being overdue. But the conversation (argument) was interrupted by a three foot little blond girl with ponytails pulling at your arm asking you to go camping. As you leave in haste, not wanting to be yelled at by Mr. "what's his name" new boss, you just keep saying to both of them "I can't, I can't, I can't." to all three requests. I can't have dinner with my family, I can't pay that stupid bill, and I can't go camping. But you can make it to work on time for Mr. Levinski, LEVINSKI, that's it! No wait, Pentinski, yeah, Pentinski...you think.

Your trip to work is filled with self-talk. "What do they want from me? I'm working so hard for them." Meanwhile, the hearts of those at home are being filled with other heroes.

Wow, no respect at home, no appreciation, and everyone seems to be someone's hero but you. Is this the way you wanted life to be? What are you going to do about it? Yes, I'm asking YOU! Getting mad and putting down the book won't help; the truth has already been exposed to your mind.

You want to be a hero, right? Well, heroes face the giants to protect those they care for. Ok, ok, I will help you; every hero has to have a sidekick, right?

First, let's look at the fight we are fighting. With logic and reason we can get a clear view of the enemy's weaknesses. What have you being doing in your fight to be a hero thus far?

Working at your job a lot...Check.
Spending more time away from loved ones than with them...Check.
Making a lot less money than you are worth...Check.
Making your "career" your priority...Check.
Making too little to make dreams come true...Check.
Climbing the "career" ladder...Check.
Working 30+ hours a week...Check.

Here's the bad news, Super Genius; EVERYTHING you are doing is CAUSING your problems.

Now, before you get all high and mighty, don't go saying "Well, money doesn't solve everything." **That is true, but the lack of it solves nothing!**

The only way what you are doing can work is if your wife said to you when you got married, "Sweetie, I want to have so little money that I have to use a sharpie to color my shoes. I want you to spend so little time with me that we don't communicate. I want to be such a stranger to you that you don't touch me, and the neighbor's plumber starts looking good. I want you to spend so little time with our daughter that she tries drugs when pressured, and she lets a boy have his way with her when she's only 15."

Hurts, doesn't it!?

Then STOP what you are doing!

You are right though; it isn't all about money. You can be a celebrity making millions or a lawyer who *takes* millions, and they can be equally as lacking when it comes to being a hero as the man who makes minimum wage. Spending 30+ hours at work and four hours with your wife and kids, what does it really say about your priorities, regardless of income?

So what makes a superhero? Well, let's look at Superman. He has super powers and the character to do the right thing. He even leaves his job as a reporter to go be a hero. You don't have the ability to look through a building or to freeze the ocean with your breath but that doesn't mean you cannot have super powers.

You will still need character. Character is your ability to define what is important to you, starting with your personal vertical alignment. You then take those priorities, your morals, and how you act in your life to defend and advance those principles: this is your character.

As for your super powers, those are the total control of your time and your money. Money gives you the ability to do things, accomplish things, and fund things. You have heard thousands of times that money makes the world go round. Well, it doesn't, but it does give you the ability to go around with it. Money is, however, almost entirely useless without the next item: Time.

Time gives you the power to put your money into action, as well as, the power to accomplish those things that money cannot do. Time is poorly spent making money; your exchange rate for time vs. money can never work in your favor. Think of it this way. You can invest time or you can spend time. When you are working for a living, you are getting paid to do it, meaning you are spending your time.

So, with this in mind, let us take a look at the start of the chapter again. This time I will paint the picture from the eyes of a hero (Hero = Character + Time + Money).

Before we do, however, let me make this point clearly. There are two types of heroes. There are heroes like the airline pilot who landed safely in the Hudson and the men and women who ran up the Twin Towers when others ran out. They are real heroes. I don't want to take away from them in any way, shape or form.

With that said, there are then two types of heroes. There are accidental heroes, which are those mentioned just prior. The guy who jumps on the hood of a car as the car is washing down a flooded river to save a baby. That man is an accidental hero. Then, there are those like the hero I want you to become who lives the life of a hero each and every day. People, for example, like Ron Puryear, Jeff Mosurinjohn, Orrin Woodward, and Bill Gates.

So in painting this picture to prove the power of what's being taught here, I will limit the amount of money in the following analogy to something very reachable for EVERY person reading this book. You could make more, much more with what I'm teaching but "enough" will work for the following re-telling of our story.

You walk down the hall, trying to be quiet. Watch out for the creaky spot in front of the bathroom. Your toes find a doll on the hallway floor. You would love to pick it up, but in your arms is a cute little blonde girl who fell asleep doing a jigsaw puzzle with her daddy. You use that foot that found the doll to open the pink door on the left. Thankfully, Dora is giving off enough light to see her bed. You lay her down softly, careful not to wake her. You sit next to her, careful now as you brush her hair out of her face. There on her night stand you see a photo of you and her holding a school project. In the photo, you are both smiling with pride. As you look around her room, you see painted above her bed:

"I am my father's daughter.
I am strong in spirit, mind, and body.
I can accomplish anything.
My parents love me and lead me with vision, wisdom and discipline."

And this painting on the wall was done with craft paint you remember helping her pick out on a daddy/daughter date a few months ago.

You make your way back down the hall. Looking over the loft railing you find your wife is not on the couch reading, which is where you last left her. A flickering glow comes from beneath your bedroom door. Opening the door so slowly and quietly, you question if it is even opening. You are not worried about waking her; you are instead trying to possibly catch a glimpse as slips into her silky night gown.

Accomplishing your goal, you find her standing between the bed and the fireplace in the same nightie you were wishing for. You think to yourself, "She is more beautiful today then the day I married her." As you move closer to hold her, she cups your face, looks you in your eyes, and says, "You are my hero. I love you more today than the day I married you." Moving closer to the bed, you have to be careful not to trip over your sleeping bag which is sitting packed and ready to go for tomorrow.

Well, big boy (or girl), it's up to you. Which one are you going to be? You can be the working slump, making everyone wealthy but his/her own family, worrying about economic collapse, health care costs, and marriage, or you can be the hero we just finished looking at— where you live your life not limited by lack of money or lack of time and with a heart full of purpose, passion and adventure.

As your sidekick I feel like I should let you in on a little secret. Get closer, I need to whisper it to you. Ready?

"Pssst, the second option is actually easier to accomplish than the first."

Seriously, it is. Don't buy the lie that we all have been told about having to be lucky or highly educated. Don't believe the lie that you can't have the life you dream of. Too many people are counting on you. Break free, hero, break free!

Chapter Eleven:

Life with a Mission

Be honest. Do you like getting up early, before your body and mind have had enough time to rest? Do you like all that unhealthy eating you do during the work week? How about the stress? Stress is the leading cause of death, so you have to be excited about stress, right? Okay, last one. Do you like the thoughts that run through your head on your way to and from work about how your work really doesn't make a difference in the world? And you question why you are even going?

That's because you have no mission in life. Why are you even here? You may be 20, 30 or 100 years old, and it's time you figure you why you wake up each day.

I believe when you have goals, a vision, and a mission, work becomes rewarding. You wake up excited about getting everything done on your list. You are making a list, right?
Not sure what your mission should be? Not motivated in life to do much of anything? No problem, we can work through this together.

Let's start with negative motivation. I'm not a huge supporter of negative motivation, but I do believe it has a place. I find it most effective with people who have become so disheartened that the fire of a dream has all but died. Negative motivation, in my opinion, works on the principle of self-protection. When you look at the work of those like Richard Bandler and how he treats schizophrenics, we notice a trend of the mind. The mind of a human has a built in, self-preservation mechanism. How does this relate to you if you have little excitement about living your life?

I think you are slightly nuts to be honest. Don't feel bad. Life in today's world has programmed you to be this way.
Try this:

Close your eyes. Count slowly backward from 10 – 1, counting on each breath out. On each breath picture someone who is using their life to live a life that others would view as significant. I'm sure you can think of one or two, but let me suggest a few for you to either use or to get your brain thinking, a spark of inspiration if you will. (A note though, before you get started. For your mental picture, chose someone who you actually know what they look like.)

If you need help:

- Rick Goad
- Lance Armstrong
- Abraham Lincoln
- Mother Theresa
- Stephen Baldwin
- Disabled athletes
- John C. Maxwell
- Tony Robbins
- Rachael Ray
- Michael Jordon

Feel free to use your own. I just listed a cross section to get you thinking. They don't have to be charity driven or a martyr, just someone who you see as living a powerful life, a life that is dedicated to a pursuit; and they wake everyday wanting to take on the day and make it happen.

Ok, got your list?

Now, as you breathe in, close your eyes. Picture in front of you this extraordinary group of people you have assembled all standing on a nice tropic beach. Take in another deep breath; hold it for a count of two. On this breath, picture yourself standing in front of them; when you breathe out, walk towards them. Now, in a state of relaxation, you feel right at home with this group. Everyone is laughing together as if someone just told a funny joke. Standing on this tropical beach with all of these people you hear music, not soft, not loud when all of a sudden all of your people start doing the chicken dance. Sounds silly, right?

Continue doing this throughout today. Take your time, go slow. Run the following scenarios in your mind with your group.

1. Eating together at a fun restaurant
2. Building a home from scratch together
3. Riding a roller coaster together
4. Putting up sand bags together in a hurricane

Now, the odds are that after the previous exercise you should not need much negative motivation. It should have flamed a bit of a spark knowing what you can do with your life. Allowing your mind to accept that it can be an equal to those of achievement tends to counter act some of the negative, reinforced lies your mind has been accepting as truth. However, if your brain needs a bit more motivation, let's look at a negatively motivated action plan.

We have already established the fact that what you are doing in life is probably not working. Reaching for the stars may be a stretch for you at this point, so telling you that you can have a life of world travel, life changing experiences, and private jets may not motivate you at this point. Go ahead and re-read the chapter "The Coming Storm" then come back here, I will hold this page for you.

Are you back? Good. Scared? Good.

When you go to bed tonight, do me a favor. Make a list of what you would like your life to be like when that storm I talk about hits. Things like: enough money so you don't have to steal or starve, a good enough car to get your family to safety, the ability to keep your marriage together by spending time with your spouse, keeping your kids off drugs, and providing care for aging parents.

You will make this list proportionate to your financial need. For example, if you have some money then spending time with your spouse or making sure you kids stay off drugs will still be on the list. You may add something like make sure your church has the means to continue, and provide support for a homeless shelter.

Okay, do you have your list? Now, when you wake up look at that list, and if you remain an employee, you know whatever is on that list will never come to pass. Before going to bed again, take that list, and if you have done nothing today to get yourself free from a job, take a red pen and cross out each item. If you can, look at your wife while you are doing it.

There is a great business man from the Northwest, his name is Dave. Dave was an inspiration to me when I was young, still is for that matter. I heard Dave say, when speaking to some business owners, "Put a check for $5,000 on your TV screen with a piece of tape, which is what you are costing your family every day you stay at your job. Now before you can watch TV you have to pull that check off."

Here's the low down on negative motivation. Lazy people don't jog. People who are motivated by the benefits of jogging: great health, sexy body, stamina in bed, and the ability to eat whatever they want-- they don't need negative motivation. On the other hand, there exists the rest of us who need the negative motivation where if we don't run, something bad will happen, diabetes or heart disease. The laziest among us would run if chased by a police dog. Big claws, big teeth, mean face, and 120 lbs of angry Rottweiler barking on your heels, and you get wings on your feet.

Look at this world, at your empty bank account, look at your empty marriage, and look at your empty relationships with family and friends.

Imagine dying and meeting the person you COULD have been.

WOOF. WOOF.

Now, for you "glass is half full" types. What the hell are you doing in a job? You have 95% of what it takes to be healthy, wealthy and wise already. I guess you need to be motivated too.

I want you to ask yourself two questions and make a list too. These questions I must admit I did not come up with, they have been floating around business circles for decades.

1. Pretend I gave you $100 million dollars and 5 years to live. What would you do? Who would you spend the time and money with? Who would you help? How would you make the world remember you were here?

2. If you KNEW and I mean knew with 100% certainty that anything you wanted to try you would be successful at, what would you spend your life pursuing? Politics? Treasure Hunting? Business? Acting?

Chapter Twelve:

The Princess and the "A" Word

B y far the most popular and the most ridiculed segment of the business world is the direct sales industry. This industry also goes by a couple other names. Multi-Level Marketing (MLM), "Private Franchising", and Network Marketing are the most common.

The direct sales industry should at least be looked at by EVERYONE who is considering starting a business. Worldwide over 62 million people own a direct sales business, and it accounts for sales in excess of $114 billion dollars. It is an industry that anyone, with any background can get involved in. To ignore such a powerhouse would be stupid.

I will admit, however, that there are negatives and misconceptions tied to these businesses. In this chapter and in the "FAQ" section of this book, I will be setting the record straight.

Since there may be a large portion of readers who are not familiar with the network marketing industry, let's look at two of the most prominent names.

MARY KAY aka "The Princess"

Mary Kay was started by American business woman, Mary Kay Ash. Mary Kay Ash had prior experience in the direct sales industry, and in 1964, she decided to offer a product line and business opportunity that has helped women and their families all over the world. Through a network of self-employed business owners, Mary Kay now does business sales in excess of $2.4 billion. They are also well known for rewarding their top performers with the legendary pink vehicles. Do you know of any woman who has never used a Mary Kay product? Neither do I.

AMWAY aka "The 'A' Word"

By far the biggest dog on the block, Amway was started in 1959 by two best friends, Rich Devos and Jay Van Andel. These two had a long history of adventure and business together. I would recommend their biographies to anyone. They too had prior experience in direct sales with a company called Nutrilite (which they later bought). Currently, Amway is operating in 90 countries & territories with sales in excess of $8.4 billion dollars.

In a nutshell, direct sales works like this: you start a business in association with a parent company (i.e. Mary Kay, Amway). You then perform two primary tasks. First, like any business that has a product or service, you sell that product or service for a profit. Most direct sales companies also have bonus and incentive programs in place to reward you for great performance in this first roll. Second, you multiply your efforts by "franchising" your system to other people who want to own a business that is partnered with the same parent company. The parent company then rewards you based on the performance of those businesses which you helped start. Think of it as a commission that is only made when you help someone else make money first. It's doing business in the form of the "golden rule."

The benefits of starting a business in the network marketing world are immense. Most direct sales businesses have very low start up costs, virtually no overhead, fast start up, developed product line(s), and the best part, an organization for teaching and mentorship.

Because most businesses these days fail due to lack of knowledge and lack of capital, direct sales businesses are ideal choices. The knowledge is provided by the people who only benefit when you grow your business, and as I just stated, these types of businesses are cheap to start, usually under $500. I have the belief that these businesses should charge more, much more, because the inexpensive cost to start a business with this much opportunity for so little tends to make people not take it seriously. However, since I do not own or run any of these companies they are priced where everyone can afford to own one. A better way to look at it is, they are priced so nobody can afford not to own one.

It is true, however, that the direct sales industry carries with it some negative perceptions. Some are just, most are a load of &*^@.

The biggest misconception is that these businesses are "Pyramid Schemes." If you are presented with a real direct sales business that is a member of the Direct Sales

Association, and you think someone is trying to get you into a pyramid scheme, you are an idiot. Read the chapter "Land of the Pharaohs". In a direct sales business your income is determined and limited by you. The best part is not only can you pass the people above you (not possible in a pyramid), but those people want you to because they make money when you make money. Matter of fact, they are there to help you accomplish that goal. Something your job not only makes impossible, but your boss doesn't want you to do better than him because it's bad for *him*.

This leads me to a related misunderstanding. It is this objection some people have that goes like this: "Well, this is just making money off of other people." DUH! If you view that as a real objection and something that may keep you from starting a direct sales business, again, you are an idiot. Sorry, I thought someone should tell you.

I'm going to take this further. If that is an objection for you, you should know you will never succeed in any business, even a non-profit. Matter of fact, you won't even do well as an employee. Every business, including non-profits, makes money off of people. At your job, your boss makes money off of you and your effort. You make money off of the company you work for's clients. If you owned a business and hired someone to work on Saturday so you could see your kids, you are making money off of that person. If you were running a charity you are making money off of your donors' hard work.

If you do find it disturbing to make money off of people, the BEST business you could ever be in is a direct sales business. In those businesses, you only make a small percentage when the person you helped to get involved in your direct sales business makes a large percentage. To make it even better, the person you got involved in the business can make as much as they want, even more than you. So in fact, you are doing something so great for them that nobody else has ever done and that is to offer them a way to gain wealth and freedom based on their own efforts. You should feel good about that and when you understand what this concept is all about you probably won't find any other business as gratifying.

The other misconception, what you "think" you know. By that, I mean you will hear people say something like "Oh, Amway, no thanks. My parents tried something like that." or "Mary Kay huh? Don't I have to go door to door?"

I find responses like this almost funny, because as a society, we have come to get used to everything changing so fast—technology, medicine, and even business changes every other day. Look at the cell phone you owned in 2005. They don't even sell anything that crappy anymore. Look at your computer. My laptop now has more memory than the largest computer in the world in 2001. Starbucks is now getting beat up by McDonalds in the coffee business! If everything else can change in an instant, don't show your stupidity by saying something like "No thanks, I saw that a few months ago." or "Gee, I was in that a year ago and it's just not for me."

While I'm on it, don't bring what you think you know to the table when looking at any business. For example, it used to be years ago that if you were involved in a direct sales business you would need to have a large inventory. Now with internet fulfillment, that requirement has all but ceased to exist.

Once you have decided to get involved in a network marketing business the next thing to do and by far the most important is get involved in the system. Most direct sales businesses have organizations, books, video, audio and events. These are your most powerful tools! Again, for some reason though there are people who question this too.

The most common objection is "Well, I heard on television that the books, videos and events are points of profit for those 'above me.'" You don't know how ridiculous you sound when you say something like that. It's funny how people think college is a great idea, and will gladly pay $89 for a $4 book. But man, if someone makes a $2 profit on a book bought at wholesale in a business situation, the world comes to an end, and that person is looked at as if he/she were a snake oil salesman. Newsflash! The college knows exactly how to suck that $85 dollars of pure markup from you, get you to pay it, and then you go brag about how much you paid as if it were a badge of honor. Ask someone who is going or who has went to college about the cost and 9 out of ten times they will show off by telling you how much they spent on books. As if the more you spent impresses those you are telling. Who's the fool again?

People object to "having to pay and attend *'those'* business functions". "Those" business functions that will help you and your family have a great life. But at the same time, they will then tell their children to spend $70,000 dollars for four years of parties and poor education which, by design, cannot make them successful. Who helps you put your pants on in the morning? These objections to people making money off of you for educating you on how to build a business would be the equivalent of opening up your own retail store, and then starting a blog talking about how your landlord is just renting you the space so he makes money off of you.

Here's the real stupidity though. Yes, those who are above you get paid for selling you a product or they get paid when you attend an event they worked hard to organize and put together. SO WHAT? You too can get paid when YOU sell a book or YOU put on an event. What a concept. It's not like they are doing something dirty or shady. It's what every business, every good business anyway, does. Do you know how crazy a sales manager would look to me if when I go in their business to train his sales team he says, "Josh, how dare you! You sold me this book; you should have told me you were going to make money off of it."

When I meet people who somehow made it to adulthood and say stuff like this I think of a great quote by Dean Kosage, "Shh, you're so pretty, don't talk."

One last thing I want to mention about the books, functions and, other tools. Don't be an idiot and say something like "I don't need that stuff, that's just a bunch of rah-rah stuff to try to get you motivated." If your child was involved in football and they were having a team meeting or a locker-room talk at half-time, would you really let him/her get away with saying something so stupid? If a child looks foolish objecting, how do you think an adult looks? Truth of the matter is, you do need to be motivated; otherwise, I would be reading *your* book right now. If whatever you have been doing up to this point in your life has been what motivated you to get to this point of your life, how on earth do you think that will take you to where you have never been? Besides, motivation is only a small part of it. Have you learned anything from this book? Well, why don't you think you will learn something from the resources others have to offer when they have done what you are trying to do? Plus, remember how I said things change so fast? Obviously, you want to succeed, so why not stay on the cutting edge? Then there is the most important aspect of plugging into the system, and that's the power of association. The power of association is a force so powerful that it would take me a whole book to cover it properly.

Bottom line is, look into direct sales. Yes, some direct sales businesses ARE better than others, so do your research. Also, read the "FAQ" section of this book. These companies can get most people to where they want to be faster and with less pain then other business options. Do yourself and your family a favor, and don't listen to your ignorant neighbor. Be your own man/woman, and remember, "I do today what others won't, so I can do tomorrow what others can't."

Chapter Thirteen:

Get Rich Slow Schemes

D id you know that in America alone there are millions of millionaires? As of 2007, Forbes reported there are 946 billionaires. Makes you really see the difference between a millionaire and a billionaire, doesn't it? Keep that in mind as we journey through this chapter.

I remember a business mentor of mine, John Gilmour once asking a room of several hundred people, "How much money do you have to make per year to be considered really well off?"

After a bit of discussion with the room, they settled on $250,000 a year. That's the amount these 500 or so people, all from different backgrounds and professions agreed would be considered a large enough income to be considered "well off."

Then he asked them a question which the answer, still, to this day astounds me. "At $250,000 per year, how long would it take you to become a billionaire?"

The answer is: 4,000 YEARS!

If you were making $250,000 a year the day Jesus was born you, would still have almost 2,000 years to go!

Pay attention to what I'm about to tell you as it goes against *everything* you have been taught and everything society tells you.

You cannot get rich slowly!

Not only is the belief that you can get rich slowly just going to limit you, but it is actually impossible. Here's why.

The cost of living doubles (at least) every ten years. The average American home 40 years ago had **one** income earner bringing in $9,350 a year . If we kept up with the cost of living (not what is reported as inflation, but the cost of living) that **one** income home would be making $74,800 in 2009. Instead the average **two** income in America in 2009 was only $50,740. That's for a TWO INCOME HOME! Meaning, to keep up, the average household income today would have to be near $140,000, not the $50,740 it is! That is why what used to be a great contribution to his retirement back then of

10% of that one income earner's weekly pay wouldn't even pay for two movie tickets today! We hear all the time the huge number we will have if we start investing in our 401ks and mutual funds when we are young. That's backwards math. Instead, it would translate like this.

What if you put $16 dollars a week away now, $8 dollars a week away ten years from now, $4 dollars a week away 20 years from now, and $2 dollars away a week 30 years from now? Would you be able to retire? Of course not, that's why people who did save and are now 60, 70, 80 year olds who are pinching pennies, losing their homes, working at the super retail outlets. With $16 dollars (approx 10% income 40 years ago) a week was a huge percentage of their income. Then ten years later that $16 became a real value of only $8, as the cost of living double, cutting in half the value of the original $16.

Let me put it another way. Unless you are getting 10% interest per year, you are making ZERO progress! If you are making less, you are going backwards. Even if you are making 20% you are not going to be rich and have the life you are dreaming of, the life that prompted you to pick up this book.

It is mathematically impossible!

Now before you start throwing out nonsense like "That's not true, inflation is only 3% a year." let me save you some embarrassment. I don't care what the FED says inflation is. First, they are lying! Second, it doesn't really matter.

In 1939, the cost of a new car was $700. If all those financial planning wizards are right about inflation, in 1949, the price would be $939.58. So what was the cost of a new car in 1949? $1,420. Well, it seems like the cost doubled (and then some) in ten years. Maybe the car industry was just a fluke. A new home in 1939 cost $3,800. Let's see what the cost of a new home was in 1949...uh oh, it was $7,450.

Sure, that was back then, but let's see if the trend continued:

If the cost of a home in 1939 was only $3,800 then the price of a new home in 1989 should only be around $16,000 (without compounding, only $9,500) but what was it? $120,000. That's about a 3,000% percent INCREASE!

Perhaps you just need a second to let that sink in.

What that means is, you can never, under any circumstances, save your way to riches! It's a lie.

I know what you hear all the time about investing your way to wealth. I know you hear about 401k and the "rule of 72." Investment "gurus" will tell you, invest young and you will be wealthy when you are 70 years old. The obvious question I have is, why not be wealthy when you are young?

Let's take a look at the math though, see how realistic this is. If you invest $5,000 a month you would need to make about $180,000 a year. It would be about a third of your PRE-TAX income. That would put you in the top 5% of income earners in the nation. Keep that in mind, because if you are not in the top 5%, your investment opportunity won't even be this bright.

You invest this $5,000 a month at the age of 35 and you keep that up for 30 years. You also need to get 10% interest per year for the entire 30 years. That's not unrealistic, is it? (That's sarcasm, by the way.) At the end of the 30 years you will have about $11 million dollars. Don't get too excited, it's only worth $2.75 million in *actual* value, as remember value of money gets cut in half every ten years.

Now, while that may sound like a lot, it really isn't. This only works for you IF you are in the top 5% income earners in the country AND you save that $5,000 per month, AND you can put away 1/3 of your monthly income. What that means is 95% of you are out by default and another 4% are out due to laziness and circumstances. Translated, it means only 1% of the people who go the route of high income employment will ever reach the high level of comfort. Not rich, just comfort.

Let's do it again, but this time we will use the average American with a realistic interest rate.

The average American makes a little over $50k a year, so a 1/3 investment from him/her would be $325 a week. You can afford to do that out of your current budget, right? (Again, notice the sarcasm.) If you could and you got 3% interest, which is pretty good, you would have at the end of 30 years a retirement nest egg with an *actual* value of $23,733. Can you live for 20-30 more years if that's all the money you have?

Put it this way. With the millions of wealthy people in the world today, zero percent of them made it there slowly. Matter of fact, to prove my point of the rapid de-valuing of money even further, there are countless news articles and television reports on how millionaires today still have to work, pay off debt, and worry about bills. I have even heard there are millionaires next door. Remember a time when a millionaire meant wealth, luxury, freedom, and carried a certain mystic about it? A millionaire in net worth these day's isn't even considered "rich" by practical standards.

So what does this mean? It means all those people who have ever told you, "Stay away from get rich quick schemes" are ignorant. How do we know this? Because...

nobody on the Forbes 400 list has been alive for 4,000 years. You can ONLY become wealthy quickly!

This is just logic.

First, we need to figure out what "rich" is. How much money do you want to make? A word of caution, it is not bad or evil to want to be rich—in money, experiences, relationships, etc. Occasionally, I will run across people who say that its greed; or they will throw out a Bible verse they don't understand. Don't buy their lie.

People who say it's wrong to be rich are the most selfish and useless people, and you should feel very sorry for them. I will give you an example. Feel free to experiment in your own life, you will find I'm correct.

If I were to ask someone who has a job if it is wrong to get a raise they would say "no." Interesting. Then, if I asked them why it's not wrong for them to get a raise I would hear:

- I am being rewarded for my hard work
- I need to pay bills
- I have worked for my education

- I deserve this raise

Notice how everything is about them.

Then if I asked them what they would do if they got a 20% raise at work I would get the following:

- I would pay off debt
- I could get a new car/TV/house
- I could send my kids to college
- I could take a vacation
- I could get tickets to the concert/sporting event

Notice again, it's all "Me, me, me, I, I, I."

THEY are the ones consumed by greed giving 30+ hours a week to someone in voluntary slavery for the crumbs they are tossed. They are selfish as they are concentrating on what they can get and how they deserve it. I know that sounds extreme and not everyone feels this way. But those who tell you it's wrong to be rich, they feel this way.

Don't argue, I'm right, and you know it.

These are the people who say ignorant things like "nobody needs that much money."

Try this: either find someone else or if you are going to use the same person, give it a few weeks then ask; "If I gave you $100 million, what would you do with it?" The top answers are usually something like this:

- I would give to the children's hospital
- I would build a homeless shelter
- I would make sure nobody in my family is ever in need
- I would bring my aging parent home and get a nurse
- I would feed the hungry

That defeats the lie that getting rich is bad. Actually getting wealthy, as long as you have common sense and any heart, is actually a selfless act. Sure, there are crooks with a lot of money who hurt people but there are poor people who hurt people too and usually FOR money.

So let's define what "rich" is.

Rich is having enough money so that money is no longer a concern and it has no control over you, your time, your experiences, or your relationships. Rich is NOT an income that pays the bills with a little left over to put in savings. Rich is NOT net worth. Net worth is 90% useless. It's only useful when you sell the asset for money. I might have a baseball card "worth" $10,000, but unless I can convince someone in the market to actually pay me for it, I can't use it to feed my kids. Look at the economic crisis of 2009 where net worth wealth was cut in half almost overnight.

I am NOT saying you shouldn't invest. Mutual funds, real estate and other investments can be good, not wealth producing per se, but good. Getting some interest is better than getting nothing.

Now that we have decided that any get rich slow scheme is a lie, how do we get rich quickly?

The power is in multiplication and that can only be done in ownership, not employment.

There are millions of ways to use the power of multiplication. But let's just look at a couple, so you get what I'm talking about.

A farmer buys 10 potato seedlings and pays .70 cents. He then gets 10 potatoes from each plant, selling each potato for .40 cents, making a profit of $39.30, a 5,614% profit in one growing season!

A software developer develops a great new program. He produces a CD with the program on it for $2.00 and sells it for $50, a 2,500% profit. What if he sells 1 million copies?

A hamburger stand franchises their program where each location produces a franchise fee and royalties of $60,000 per year per location and they sell the rights to 1,000 locations making $60,000,000. An amount they could never have made by just having one restaurant.

The greatest investment you can make in any business is investing in people. People allow you to multiply your efforts. None of these previous examples would produce wealth if the business owner didn't also invest in people.

The potato farmer would need to hire people to run a farm big enough to produce wealth, even if he planted and picked 24 hours a day, he can only do so much. If he has ten people working 8 hours a day, he gets 80 hours of labor in a 24 hour day!

The software programmer and the hamburger franchiser also will go nowhere without multiplying the people factor. This plays a huge role in choosing your course of action in business.

This means that if you and your husband have the idea of opening a flower shop in Walla Walla, Washington, you should know right now, you will never be rich. Also, even if you do earn a decent income, you will not control your time. You will have to spend your productive time and energy running your flower shop.

On the other hand, if you want to be in the flower business AND be rich, your action plan from the beginning needs to be either franchising, so you can have hundreds of locations from coast to coast selling flowers or a few dozen distribution hubs around the country to sell mainly on-line and/or through call in ordering.

That's using the power of multiplication to allow you to sell millions of flowers a week.

Your ability to arrange flowers better than the next guy does no good in business. Every local restaurant makes a hamburger better than the burger joint with the red haired clown, but who makes more money?

Speaking of that red haired clown's burger joint, you can ask yourself, "Who makes the most money, the guy who buys the one franchise or the family that sells the franchising rights?"

So to recap, getting rich quickly is the only way to get rich. Those who tell you to stay away from "get rich quick" plans are either broke or ignorant.

Most importantly invest first and foremost in people and business actions that are designed to be executed through multiplication.

Chapter Fourteen:

Those Who Came Before Us

It's always a good idea to see that other people have done what you want to do. In this chapter, I'm going to profile a few of my favorite business people.

Daniel Snyder: This guy drops out of school and starts a business chartering jets for college kids who are going on spring break. He runs the business out of a bedroom and rumor has it, he made a million dollars with this "side business." Now, he owns Johnny Rockets, Snyder Communications, Six Flags, and my favorite, the Washington Redskins. Daniel Snyder is the perfect example of creative, strategic entrepreneurship.

Micky Jagtiani: Drops out of school and becomes just another average taxi driver in London until he starts his own business. He takes his infant supply store and turns it into an empire .Which today, has given him a wallet with $2.5 billion in it. He now spends his money and time helping orphanages in India.

JR Simplot: This gentleman died in 2008, but is still by far one of the best examples of what passion and logic can produce. He dropped out of school at the age of 14 and started his own business. That was in 1923. For those of you not familiar with American history, research the 1920's and 1930's, and see what the economic conditions were like back then.

This teenager was more successful in business than all the over-educated, Ivy League geniuses. Matter of fact, Mr. Simplot and the example he left behind almost served as the title of this book; "Potatoes vs. Ivy: How a Simple Farm Kid Can Teach You More About Wealth Than Any College."

How did this young man make a multi-billion dollar fortune? Farming. You see, in hard times established businesses, those with debt and heavy infrastructure, sell off assets. Pig farmers will sell off hogs for pennies on the dollar, and crop growers are more than eager to negotiate strategic business situations.

If you have ever eaten a French fry at McDonalds you have experienced JR Simplot's business.

Richard Schulze: Talk about the perfect example of using logic, reason, and passion. Mr. Schulze is the founder of Best Buy. I'm sure you have heard of it. The company does very well, if you call $45 billion in revenue pretty good. He's married, has ten children— yes, ten— which means that $3 billion he has in the bank account probably comes in handy. Oh, before I forget, did I mention he only has a high school diploma? Well done, Mr. Schulze!

Big John Lipscomb: The one man on this list who reminds me most of Mr. Simplot. Big John was sick and tired of the "system," so he decided to take his family, move to the middle of nowhere in Montana, and live in a straw house. Smartest decision he has ever made. With his family relationships solid, he decides to sell seeds (SurvivalistSeeds.com). He spends a couple hundred dollars on advertising and—bam! — About one year later he is a millionaire. He then takes that same logic and reason and starts a number of other companies. Very outspoken about the state of things, Big John will serve as an example of what a smart businessman can be for generations to come (if there are generations to come— right, John?)

Terry Felber: I have known Terry for over a decade now. His path runs so close to my own, it's crazy.

Starting with a fishing boat operation in Alaska to involvement in dozens of other businesses, Terry is one of the most complete business men in America today.

Terry now spends his time helping thousands of other people create wealth around the world. He also is strong in his Christian faith, and uses his marketplace ministry to not only advance the faith but to teach on the relationship between religion and money. He is the author of two books, "Am I Making Myself Clear?" and "The Legend of the Monk and the Merchant." Both are foundational and inspiring. I strongly urge everyone to read both.

Michael Powell: Owner of Powell's Books, one of the largest book stores on and off the internet. He started his business very creatively through consignment situations.

Mr. Powell did an interview for this book and addressed issues that most of you will soon be facing as you start businesses. His understanding of how to blend management of employees while still focusing on the business' purpose is pure gold. His example of being David versus Goliath is equally amazing. He realized what his competitive advantage was against stores like Barnes and Noble and Borders, and has been successful at taking advantage of their weaknesses.

He also has a firm grasp around passing on his business to his daughter, Emily. The insight I gained in the interview is the foundation of a future book I'm releasing about the continuation of businesses to successive generations.

Mr. Powell knows how to think strategically in business, and it's no wonder why he is one of America's best business leaders.

Riley Livingston: Riley is a great example of determination. He was an employee of a health and wellness company when a series of events led him to believe he could run a similar business better. As with most people who venture out into the world of business ownership, his family was 100% against it. They wanted Riley to go the route of education and good employment.

Luckily for them, Riley decided to be his own man and forge ahead as a business owner. He opened two companies; the most noted is Zipfizz, an energy drink additive you can combine with the beverage of your choice.

Riley's brave move turned into a yearly revenue stream in the tens of millions. Making him a great example of what can be done with will and determination.

My hope is this list helps you to see that you can, regardless of background, nationality, or political view points, take advantage of free enterprise.

Chapter Fifteen:

First Things First

Everyone wants to know what they do for their life's work makes a difference. Yes, we can go down the trail of "It's a Wonderful Life" and say that everyone impacts everyone else. Yes, if you were never born the world would be a different place. While I'm glad you are alive, let's get real for a second. If you are an employee, there is a huge chance that what you do for a job really doesn't matter. You could die tomorrow. Everyone would be sad, but the business wouldn't slow down. You would be replaced by the end of the week, maybe two weeks if you are an executive.

When I was selling cell phones we used to say, "We are not curing cancer." and it was so true. If I sold a phone, nothing good happened. If I didn't sell a phone, nothing bad happened. Yes, the phone made a profit for the company and the share holders, but you know what I mean. I was completely replaceable by someone else who could sell the phone. Sure, the phone could be used later that day to call 911 to report a drunk driver and save the lives of all the nuns on the bus but that had nothing to do with my life's mission. Whatever you are doing for your job probably doesn't either. There are always exceptions, for example: doctors and nurses. Their work does make a difference, but even in cases like that, they're better served being either self-employed or sub-contracted.

Wouldn't you like to have a life that has impact, which creates a better situation not only for you and your family but also for your community and nation? Your nation (regardless of where you live) needs you. The world economy is fragile. Moral decay is now epidemic and the world's dreamers are dying.

There is hope, and it begins with YOU.

Here's the process:

- First, you need to talk with yourself, God, your spouse and/or anyone else that is important in your everyday life and start to awaken the dream again. Find out what moves you, what dream did you give up because you thought it was "just a dream?"

- Second, you need to do some research. Starting with deciding what kind of life you want, then research what kind of business ventures provide those lifestyle results.

- Third, step out of your comfort zone and start your business. Full time or part-time it is up to you and your situation. I know many who work their own business part-time and now, net many millions per year. This is why it's important to pick the right business vehicle. Would you rather spend 80 hours a week owning a business that nets you $40,000 a year or work 25 hours a week on a business that nets you $400,000 a year?

- Work on yourself. Eat up all the self-help and self-improvement material as if you were starving. If you are involved in a business vehicle that has resources for self growth available, buy it all. It's an amazing investment. In another chapter, I show how this form of teaching is many times more valuable than any formal education you can get.

- Spread your dream to others, starting with your family. Tell your kids what you are doing and why you are doing it. Let everyone catch the vision, and remember to share your goals and rewards for everyone in your family to enjoy.

- As your business grows, expand your influence. Let the community know what you are doing and what you stand for. Don't be afraid or ashamed of getting yourself out there. Taking a stand affects your culture allowing you to finally have an impact on the very thing that has been impacting you. We have seen the results over the past 50 years when great men and women aren't there to impact the culture.

- Start using your business to help others. Meaning, if you can franchise your business, do it. If you need to hire people, do it in a way that frees them, not confines them. (Read my upcoming book "Mind Your Own Business.")

- If you are seeking investors or business partners don't be afraid to share the vision and dream that you have. Yes, you will get some rejection; don't let it bother you. Odds are the listener who says "no" is just someone who has died in their spirit.

The truth of the matter is small business is what's going to save your nation. There is no government official that can have the impact you can. Not to mention, government officials usually don't have the heart that a small business owner has. No President, King or Prime Minister in any fancy office in any country has the same amount of power that a man or woman with a dream has in a common living room or coffee shop.

Take for example, the direct sales industry. These are businesses like The Fuller Brush Company, ACN Digital Phone Services, and Advocare. Business in this category are a business owners dream (see Chapter "The Princess and the A-Word") if you have little experience or limited capitol.

According to the Direct Sales Association, there are over 25,000,000 people who own a direct sales business. One by one, family to family, nation to nation, these business owners have been impacting and changing lives the world over.

I actually owe a lot of my passion for what I do today to what I have seen and experienced in the direct sales industry. I was 19 years old, owned a direct sales "franchise," and I was sitting across the table from a nice, middle aged couple. I spent about 45 minutes with them, talking about what really matters in life and sharing with them my option to help them have more out of life. All of a sudden, they started crying (the man first), and I was a bit taken back. When I asked why they were crying they said that they had been praying for something to come along that could set them free and that they could do with their family. Their relationship got better, their parenting got better (When kids see their parents chasing a vision, its powerful.) and of course, the fact they owned a business was helping the economy.

This is just one of dozens of stories I personally have. Divorces that didn't happen, and suicides that didn't happen are common reports when people are awakened to a life of truth and hope.

This is not just limited to my experience in the direct sales industry either. I, and many others, have cases from other entrepreneurial options that are equally as powerful. I bring up the direct sales industry simply because it's the largest option; and the one by its very design that possesses the ability to make the most positive impact on the most people the fastest and with long lasting results.

I will give you another example:

There was a man who invented a product to replace sugar. Easily packaged, cheaper to produce, and a great alternative. To my understanding, he went from hotel bar to hotel bar seeking investors from traveling businessmen. Yes, most people he came across said "no," but enough of them said "yes" that I could take you to any restaurant in the civilized world and we could probably see his product.

More importantly though, imagine the lives of the people smart enough to say "yes."

There you are, sitting in a hotel bar on yet another business trip for your boss. In your hand is a bottle of liquid relief for the pain in your soul— a cold hotel room, a strange city, kids that don't know you, parents that are lucky to get a card on holidays, bills beyond belief and a spouse who may be having an affair. But hey, don't forget your boss is proud of you. The same boss who is on his third marriage hasn't seen his grandchildren because of his estranged relationship with his daughter.

Life is just peachy.

Then some guy comes along with a little packet of sugar alternative. He tells you how an investment now can yield part ownership of his company and how he sees his product in every restaurant on the planet. You take his card, head to bed but you can't sleep. What is this feeling that's keeping you awake? You are starting to dream again. Holidays with your parents, a spouse who can't seem to keep their hands off you, and a home where you really want to live with a bed you actually get to sleep in. Those who really did say yes to this man are millionaires now, if not billionaires, but that's not the point.

The point is that it was a small business owner, just like you are about to become that changed the very lives of the people in those hotel bars.

What will make you or break you is something which is talked about less and less these days, and the result of its absence is evident. What I'm talking about is your vertical alignment. As this may be a foreign term to you, let me give you perhaps the most well known proclamation of a vertical alignment.

The U.S. Marine Corps' Vertical Alignment:

- God
- Corps
- Country

Their vertical alignment is a priority list which guides their operational foundations, affecting each and every Marine on a daily basis. For example, to a Marine, God is his/her first priority and next, the Corps, not the country, which may sound odd or even treasonous. The Corps is second, meaning the United States could crumble into the sea and the Marines would still be united and accountable to each other, standing firm. Third is country. Country being third does not mean that it is not important, far from it. There is a vital point for you here when you make your own vertical alignment. By the Marine placing God and Corps above Country, it lets him give his best to Country. His belief in God makes him a moral and accountable person, providing him with the foundation and tools to be his best for number #2.

Being a Marine gives him the ability and background to be the best he can be to serve #3.

If his vertical alignment was Country, Corps, God—he would be poor at his job, poor in his development of his manhood, and the Marines could cease to exist. Let's say that the country went the way of drugs and prostitutes. The Marine, placing country first, goes along with the flow; the Corp would be plagued with moral decay and performance incompetence, thus not being able to defend the nation. This would lead to a complete failure to his commitment of his number one priority, country.

Lack of a proper vertical alignment is the cause of most of the world's problems. Figuring out what yours is and helping those who work with you figure out what theirs is 95% of the determining factor when it comes to success in business, relationships, and life itself.

A celebrity who is suffering from drugs, wasteful spending, too much partying and bizarre behavior; a pastor who steals the offering; a governor who is busted with a hooker; a banking tycoon busted for a ponzi scheme—these are all the result of not holding to a vertical alignment. While having a vertical alignment will not make you perfect and you will still make mistakes, the lack of one guarantee a ride to failure, depression, and a life you don't want to die having lived.

So how do you get one?

You have to first list all the things that are important to you. The most common (and yours can be different) are God, spouse, kids, country, family, business, dog or whatever.

When you have your alignment parts listed, then you have to figure out which one goes where. Let's say to move your ship you have to raise anchor. The anchor is the last thing on a long chain. The problem, however, is the hole in the ship where the anchor chain comes up is cut in such a way that a link can only go in one direction; and if you have ever seen a chain, you will know that every other link is going the other direction from the one it's connected to. In raising your anchor you have to make sure one link makes it through in order to raise it enough for the next link to make it through and so on until you raise your entire chain high enough where the anchor is now at its highest point. So too is it with your vertical alignment and the example of the Marine.

What's a good example of a good vertical alignment?

- God
- Spouse
- Children
- Country
- Business

Yours may be different and this is only an example. I do not have the space in this book, nor do I want to go off on that long of a tangent to explain how to figure out which priority goes where. I have other resources (books, videos, seminars) as do many others who can help you in figuring out the order. The point is, get your list, put it in the order that fits your soul and goals and stick to it. Living a life in line with your vertical alignment is not always easy, and it requires that you make a conscious effort to pursue perfection.

Perfection this side of Heaven is not possible, but the pursuit of it is. Jeff Mosurinjohn once told me, "The definition of hell is when you die, meeting the person you COULD have been." Ouch! He was correct when he also told me, "Everything you do will either take you closer to or further from your goal." He is absolutely right. Where you buy gas and what food you eat all become important decisions when you live a life with a mission. For example: eating fast food too much not only takes you further from the goal of having an active lifestyle, but it also effects your ability to think quickly which is key in business negotiations. Knowing what we know about that, a trip to the quickie burger joint can actually affect you getting a bigger home.

It takes effort and you need to make this lifestyle just that, a lifestyle, a habit. You are not perfect, and neither am I. I will continue to be there for you though, through my books and seminars; and like I said, there are other great resources out there too.

We started this chapter by talking about the butterfly effect in "It's a Wonderful Life," (which was about a business owner, by the way). Now it's time for YOUR life to affect the world. Millions of people are crying out for an answer, you hold the power. It won't be easy, but it will be fun and well worth it.

Conclusion

W hat a book, huh?

So our journey has come to an end...for now.

My sincere hope is that not only has this book taught you something, but more importantly, I hope it causes change in your life; and that change will have a ripple effect and create not only a better economy but the environment for a better world.

I know you may be full of excitement right now. Don't let that excitement die. Act on it NOW! Take out a piece of paper and start dreaming. Start planning. Write down your priorities, goals and vertical alignment. Do your research and find the business model and opportunity that works best for you.

Don't let others take away your excitement or kill your dream. Understand that "nay sayers" just don't get it. Instead of letting them take away your treasure, give them a copy of this book; I will gladly set them straight for you.

As you learn, experience, and grow, you will undoubtedly make some rich advances in all areas of your life. If you have children, please allow them to have a leg up to your level of understanding. Culture and schooling can do a lot of damage and stump your child's growth in the areas of dreaming, accomplishment, chasing a goal and business ownership. With that in mind, don't let anyone limit your children. Encourage them daily and include them in your mission.

I also understand there may be some very smart and wise business men and women who use this book as a tool to help *you* and to share an opportunity of some sort. THANK THEM! They care about you more than your boss (probably) and they were smart enough to provide you with a great resource for you to have the life you truly want. The person who gave you this book would probably be a better business partner than a billionaire investor!

Also, I want to thank *you*. I am honored to have had the opportunity to share this time with you. If I were to give you some advice, don't let failure stop you. Thomas Edison took 1,000 tries to invent the light bulb, which means he failed 999 times. Your first go at business may fail, so what? Your job is guaranteed to fail and look at all the hopeless sheep that are sacrificing everything life has to be in that messed up situation. I, myself, have failed many more times than I have succeeded. Michael Jordan missed more than made it, and Babe Ruth is the strikeout king. **Failure is just as important to your success as success is!**

If failure does happen on your first time out, welcome to a very elite club. While you may fail, don't confuse failure with losing. As long as you never stop trying, you will never lose.

In conjunction with failure, don't let your past stop you either. I don't care if you spent the last 30 years in prison; it doesn't stop you or even slow down your ability to do great in business. I know people's past tends to stop them; don't fall victim to that lie.

There are many great resources in the world, and I highly recommend that you use them. I welcome you to all that I am doing as well.

Most importantly though, congratulations.

You would have to be dead to not be ready to start a business after reading this book. So again, congratulations. You have made a decision for you and your family. A life of purpose and adventure await you.

On behalf of the 6+ billion people on this planet that benefit from you being a business owner:

Thank You.

See you on the beaches of the world.

Frequently Asked Questions

Q: You are telling everyone to quit their job. Wouldn't that ruin the country and the world if there were no employees?

A: No. But that's not really a practical answer. The truth of the matter is that even though there will be many who start businesses after reading this book there will still be those who decide not to. They will be stopped by doubt, fear, or ego. In addition, I think people should have a job until they can break free. If I even get one percent of the population to take on self employment, the world will be a much better place.

Q: Isn't this just a bit risky to quit your job and start a business?

A: Nope. What you should do is start your first business while you are at your job. That way you still have the false sense of security to help you sleep at night until you create your own source of income.

Q: I have been on your website and see you talk about politics, and to be honest, I don't agree with everything you say about politics or religion. Why should I listen to you?

A: You don't have to. Let me ask you a question though. If you needed heart surgery would you discredit the surgeon's ability if you found out he didn't vote for the same person you did? Would you stop taking your car to a mechanic if he went to a different church than you? Only an idiot would let the fact that I may have differing points of view on other issues stop them from taking what is in this book, thinking it through and acting upon it. Should I have hidden this information from you if I knew you didn't share *my* view?

Q: I have employees and this book has been talked about a lot in the office. What should I do?

A: Embrace it. I will let you in on a little secret that I will be talking about in my next book. If you want great employees, the ones who want to quit (which is most of them) can be your best employees if you know how to take advantage of the situation. If you need help on how to manage employees in this new economy, I am available for coaching.

Q: I didn't graduate from high school. Does this mean I would be a bad business owner?

A: No, nothing could be further from the truth. Some of the most successful business owners in this country don't have much of a formal education.

Q: You have a chapter dedicated to direct marketing but no chapters really on the other types of businesses to start. Why not?

A: There are thousands of books talking about what types of businesses you can start. The point of this book was much more important than that. This book was put together to change the way people live. As far as why I gave direct marketing its own chapter, it is because I believe, if done correctly, direct marketing can be one of the best options for someone starting their first business.

I could have written a book called "50,000 Ways to Make an Extra $50,000." I almost added a chapter to this book, "Franchises, Farms, and Start-ups...Oh, My." It's my belief, however, that if I suggested certain businesses then the readers would limit their thinking to those businesses. What I want to have happen is your imagination run wild, using the foundation of vertical alignment and your personal dreams.

One of the things that separate those of wealth and those who fail in business is your ability to think "outside the box." If I were to suggest one type of business, it may impede your imagination.

Q: I was talking to my family and friends about my desire to start a business. Some laughed and others thought it was stupid. What should I do?

A: Do you want to live the life that your friends and family have? Do you want them to be stuck in the lives they have? If the answer is no, then it's up to you to be the one that breaks the chain of captivity. Leaders are leaders, because they are leaders. Think about that.

Now, if the family member who is not supportive is a spouse, tread lightly. Share, dream, and come up with goals and passions. Then, give him/her a copy of this book. It may take time, but be persistent with your spouse—for your sake and theirs.

Q: I was thinking about getting involved with a network marketing company, but then, I went on the internet and found some negative stuff about the company and certain people in the industry. What do you have to say about that?

A: Remember the saying, "There's no such thing as a stupid question?" They were wrong. Did you get your parents' permission to write in?

Look, there is negative about everything on the internet. While a small percentage may hold some merit, most of it is a bunch of whiners who would rather excuse away their failure than to truly help someone have a better life.

More importantly though—so what? Can you find anything negative with the place you work? Can you find anything negative with your best friend? Can you find anything negative about yourself? Just because there IS negative doesn't mean the opportunity itself is negative. I hope you are grown up enough to understand that.

As for the fact that there are people in an organization that may have faults or may have done something wrong, grow up.

If you live in a city with more than one person in it, there is someone in your city that did something terribly negative. Does that mean people shouldn't move to your city or do business there? I knew a guy in the military that ran a red light. Does this mean the military is bad? I knew a man who cheated on his wife with a woman he met at a health club; does this mean going to a health club would be a bad thing?

See how stupid you look when logic and reason are invited into the conversation? Don't worry, I was that way at one time, and if I can get past it, you can too.

CPSIA information can be obtained at www.ICGtesting.com
Printed in the USA
BVOW041215210413

318688BV00011B/71/P